JOURNEY TO FREEDOM
Study Guide Series

D1564764

JOURNEY

TO A LIFE OF
SIGNIFICANCE

Freedom from Low Self-Worth

YMCA OF MIDDLE TENNESSEE
SCOTT REALL

THOMAS NELSON
Since 1798

NASHVILLE DALLAS MEXICO CITY RIO DE JANEIRO BEIJING

Published in Nashville, Tennessee, by Thomas Nelson. Thomas Nelson is a registered trademark of Thomas Nelson, Inc.

Thomas Nelson, Inc. titles may be purchased in bulk for educational, business, fund-raising, or sales promotional use. For information, please e-mail SpecialMarkets@ThomasNelson.com.

Scripture references marked NKJV are from, THE NEW KING JAMES VERSION. © 1982 by Thomas Nelson, Inc. Used by permission. All rights reserved.

Scripture references marked NIV are from HOLY BIBLE: NEW INTERNATIONAL VERSION®. NIV®. ©1973, 1978, 1984 by International Bible Society. Used by permission of Zondervan Publishing House. All rights reserved.

Scripture references marked KJV are taken from KING JAMES VERSION.

To find a YMCA near you, please visit the following Web sites:

United States of America: www.ymca.com
Canada: www.ymca.ca
England: www.ymca.org.uk
Australia: www.ymca.org.au

Visit www.restoreymca.org for more information on Restore, a life-changing ministry of the YMCA.

ISBN 978-1-4185-0770-1

Printed in the United States of America.
08 09 10 11 RRD 5 4 3 2 1

CONTENTS

Caught in a downward spiral, Joan[I] came to Restore Ministries for help. Though she had a successful career and was athletic, intelligent, and attractive, she believed she was unlovable, ugly, and flawed. Joan's struggle with low self-worth began in childhood and became a lifelong burden that caused her to seek solace in self-destructive addictions. These addictions were Joan's attempt to silence her inner critic. But instead of providing comfort, her addiction actually caused Joan to feel an overwhelming sense of toxic shame. She hated herself and, eventually, took her own life.

How could low self-worth destroy such a beautiful and successful woman that, from the outside, seemed to lead a perfect life?

After watching Joan struggle with low self-worth, I realized the depth and magnitude of its power to destroy lives. This is why I wanted to begin the *Journey to Freedom* study guide series with the topic of low self-worth. At Restore Ministries, our counseling center and *Journey to Freedom* small group programs attract people from every socio-economic group, with each person dealing with a wide range of concerns including depression, codependency, loneliness, pornography, grief, loss, overspending, eating disorders, and substance abuse. All these issues stem from low self-worth. Because low self-worth drives us *almost without thought* to seek relief anywhere we can find it, we turn to alcohol, drugs, pornography, bad relationships, binging, purging—anything to make the feeling subside, if only for a moment.

Low self-worth is the overwhelming feeling that we are hopelessly broken or flawed. Most of us make mistakes and get beyond them, but people with low self-worth internalize the mistake and berate themselves for not being perfect. Usually at the heart of low self-worth is a feeling of being less than perfect. When we beat ourselves up over our mistakes, it affects every aspect of our lives and erodes our joy. If we can't live with ourselves, life will be very painful, no matter what happens externally throughout our lives.

For most of my life, I've struggled with low self-worth. I felt I had to be the best athlete in school and beyond. If I didn't outperform everyone else, I felt less than perfect and feared people would discover how inadequate I really was at the core. When sports failed to boost my self-worth, I turned to addictive behaviors and wrong relationships to kill the pain of feeling flawed. My relentless pursuit of self-worth damaged my relationships with family, friends, and coworkers. I was afraid they would discover my flaws and would not love me, but I never revealed my feelings of worthlessness. I lived as an imposter, constantly covering up, always afraid someone was going unearth my flaws.

Dr. Paul Tournier, a renowned Swedish psychiatrist, writes in *The Strong and the Weak:* "Even the most gifted, even those who claim to be surest of themselves, have a vague feeling that their reputation does not correspond to reality, and they are fearful of the fact of being observed. The most learned professor is afraid of being questioned on something he does not know. . . . The most eloquent theologian is afraid that the doubts that still haunt him will be guessed at."[2] Each of us feels a sense of weakness, but when this weakness limits our interaction with the world and those in it, when it keeps us from taking risks, it has crossed over into toxic self-doubt.

I see a lot of people who attend Restore Ministries' small groups who are consumed with this toxic self-doubt that creates low self-worth. I know people who live in pain because of low self-worth, even though they've overcome life-controlling addictions. I know people who've achieved financial freedom and are considered successful but still feel worthless. I even know some who have great families but lack fulfillment. They allow low self-worth to taint every aspect of life. It's almost like holding a balloon under water: you can keep it down through various efforts, but it will eventually surface. Low self-worth can result in painful consequences.

What we say *to* ourselves *about* ourselves is one of the most powerful tools we possess. We can create our own reality because we are in control of our attitudes. We can pull ourselves down and lead "lives of quiet desperation" simply because we don't believe in ourselves, or we can change our thoughts and live happy, healthy lives.

The first goal on the journey to freedom is to believe in the possibility of change. Everyone has the potential to secure a lifetime of hope, health, and happiness. Change is available to everyone. You can defeat low self-worth. The pain *can* subside. The first step toward this goal is to concentrate on making life *better*, not *perfect*. Avoid the idea that self-worth is a matter of perfection. In this process, we will learn new principals to live by, which means we will be less than perfect at times. The reason most people drop out of a program of change is because they feel like permanent failures, that they will never be able to change. But remember: Mistakes are not fatal. Problems are only temporary. Self-worth is yours to develop. No one can rob you of this achievement but you.

You can learn to redefine yourself. You can come to believe in the inherent goodness that God has placed in all of us and learn to identify the special gifts and talents that are uniquely yours. You can begin to see yourself as a beautiful person with unlimited potential. You can love yourself and develop a healthy self-worth.

CHAPTER ONE

WHO WE THINK WE ARE

"For as he thinks in his heart, so is he."
PROVERBS 23:7 NKJV

A therapist recently told me a story about a woman who'd allowed her absentee father—who was also an addict—to define her self-worth. Growing up, she felt that his leaving had something to do with her not being good enough. If she'd just been perfect, she believed, then he would've stayed. Through therapy, she came to realize that his leaving had nothing to do with her and everything to do with him being an addict.

Many who have attended our programs over the years have suffered with chronic low self-worth. They've felt inferior for a long time, not knowing their low self-worth could be rooted in their childhoods, much as the woman the therapist described. Some have carried a sense of inadequacy in their hearts for years, believing they'd never amount to anything.

Often in our childhoods, people in authority over us—parents, teachers, coaches—tell us we will never be good enough. Many of us have also suffered different forms of abuse as children. Physical, sexual, emotional, spiritual, or verbal abuse can make us feel broken at the core. We believe the lie: "I'm not good enough, I'm not loveable, and I'm not worth much." These deep feelings of shame and guilt can lead to a host of issues in our lives. Perhaps most damaging of all, we can allow these lies to define us as fundamentally flawed and broken. Learning to define ourselves correctly is one of the key principals of self-acceptance. As the proverb says, "For as he thinks in his heart, so *is* he."[1]

IMMEDIATE GOALS CAN BOOST SELF-WORTH

Charlie Brown is at bat. *Strike Three!*

He has struck out again and slumps over to the bench. "Rats! I'll never be a big-league player. I just don't have it. All my life I've dreamed of playing in the big leagues, but I know I'll never make it."

Lucy turns to console him. "Charlie Brown, you're thinking too far ahead. What you need to do is set yourself more immediate goals."

Charlie Brown looks up. "Immediate goals?"

Lucy says, "Yes. In the next inning, when you go out to pitch, see if you can walk out of the mound without falling down!"

Maybe you feel a little like Charlie Brown. Maybe you're down on yourself.

When low self-worth cripples our ability to enjoy relationships and endeavors, we should listen to Lucy's advice and not think too far into the future. We should set more immediate goals.

Try it. It could be as simple as showing up at the gym, or increasing your reps in a daily exercise, or attending a group meeting that focuses on your area of concern. Maybe you should make an appointment with a counselor who can begin helping you sort through your problem. Immediate goals help us feel progress. Without them, we can feel hopeless like Charlie Brown.

SELF-WORTH DOESN'T EQUAL PERFECTIONISM

Sometimes we can get self-worth and perfectionism confused with one another. Desiring excellence in our lives is a rewarding goal, but it doesn't assure we will be perfect at everything. Perfectionism has a lot to do with how we believe others perceive us. No one wants to look or act stupid. But when perfectionism causes us to continually replay past mistakes, it is toxic.

Years ago, during his presidential term, Dwight Eisenhower was vacationing in Denver. It came to his attention that a six-year-old boy named Paul Haley was dying of an incurable cancer and had one great dream—to someday meet the president. Upon hearing this, Eisenhower decided to go see young Paul Haley.

The presidential limousine arrived at the little boy's house, and out stepped the president who knocked on the door himself. Donald Haley, the father, answered the door wearing blue jeans and an old dirty shirt. He stood raggedly in front of the president with a two-day beard. The president asked for Paul.

Little Paul walked around his father's legs and looked up into the face of the man he admired the most. Dwight Eisenhower kneeled down, shook his hand, and took him out to see the presidential limousine. Before saying good-bye, the president hugged little Paul Haley. They shook hands again, and Eisenhower left.

The Haley family and the whole neighborhood were so excited about the visit. But one man was not entirely happy—Donald Haley, Paul's father. He couldn't get over the fact that he met the President of the United States when he didn't look his best!

The father's response to the president's visit seems absurd in light of his son's dying wish coming true. How could his mind be so self-focused? How did he miss the big picture? Shame can always keep us from enjoying precious moments because of some perceived failure on our part. The father should've been thrilled like his neighbors, but he only remembered his dirty clothes and unshaven face.

Shame causes us to regurgitate old mistakes, which further fuels low self-worth. It can make us feel like permanent failures. It can leave us hopeless.

SELF-WORTH IS A MATTER OF PERCEPTION

The way to overcome the self-defeating behavior of giving up is to train, not try. Training and trying are two very different things. In his book *The Life You've Always Wanted*, John Ortberg writes, "Spiritual transformation is not a matter of trying harder, but of training wisely. . . . There is an immense difference between training to do something and trying to do something."[2] When we try to change and do not succeed, we tend to give up after just a few attempts. But when we train to do something, we set our minds on learning and progressing. No matter how many times we fall short, we persevere, understanding that we are one step closer to succeeding.

Training is the key to reaching every goal. A weightlifter progresses toward his goal weight by training his muscles every day. If he fails, he trains his muscles until they exert the power needed to reach the desired goal. Ortberg writes, "Trying hard can accomplish only so much . . . you will have to enter into a life of training."[3] Trying is the raw use of willpower, nothing more. Training is learning about the life skills needed to make a change.

Achieving your ideal weight doesn't happen overnight. Finding the right career path may take years of training. Success does not mean being a perfect person. Success is learning our special purpose in life, and then training to fulfill it.

Melissa's Story

Melissa Osterloo, a 23-year-old employee of the YMCA, grew up in a poverty-stricken family of nine, where the atmosphere was often abusive. She played parent to her younger siblings and resented her parents for not stepping up more. "I remember there were times when I'd get so frustrated and hurt because when I would cry, no one would be there—there was nobody to tell me everything would be okay. All I heard were insults.

"I struggled with my weight—I was always heavy—and I got teased not only by kids at school, but also by my own family. I remember hearing awful, awful things coming out of my parents' mouths. And I think in some way they were trying to help me get control of my weight. But it just made matters worse.

"I went away to college and thought everything would get better—but it didn't. My eating spiraled out of control. During my sophomore year in college, I hit 250 pounds, and I felt like I was the worst person in the world. I felt like God didn't love me because I was heavy and I was abusing this temple He had created. I felt like I was unlovable by any human—who would love a 250 pound, 5'3" girl? I felt ugly and disgusting, and nothing I did made it better. I just kept hitting that brick wall."

After her marriage a few years later, Melissa saw that her struggle with food was not ending. Her husband, Adam, though a godly man, was not able to change Melissa's view of herself. She began to realize that she would need help if she ever hoped to see herself as God saw her.

WHAT WE TELL OURSELVES ABOUT OURSELVES

When we constantly tell ourselves that we are unworthy, we formulate a negative self-identity. Charlie Brown talks himself into a vicious cycle of self-loathing. He tells himself that he will never be a big-league baseball player, that he'll never be a person of worth. By doing this, Charlie Brown sabotages himself. He doesn't look for a solution. Rather, he identifies himself with his failure. Henry David Thoreau once said that as long as a person stands in his own way, everything seems to be in his way.

Are you sabotaging your self-worth? What's keeping you from building self-worth? Ask yourself: *Can I overcome the problems I face?* People who possess a healthy self-worth will see their problems as temporary setbacks. They will find solutions instead of turning their failures inward.

Looking back, I think I was a lot like Charlie Brown, despite the ways my parents, coaches, and teachers spoke positively into my life. Somehow I managed to create a negative definition of myself, always feeling as if I wasn't good enough. In certain settings, I experienced deep-rooted insecurity and shame. I was running *from* this deep-rooted shame more than I was running *toward* some kind of greatness. The motivation in my life wasn't a positive motivation of moving toward a goal. Instead, I ran from the fear of failure.

I was afraid someone would discover that I wasn't perfect and didn't measure up, so I tried to remain one step ahead of being discovered as a fraud. I talked a good game. I put up so many walls that it would take someone years to discover that my confidence was only veneer, with an interior of inferiority lurking beneath.

There is an enormous difference between pursuing goals in our lives and running from the fear of failure. When we pursue goals, we are motivated and have a plan of action for accomplishing those goals. But when we run from fear or failure, we never attempt greatness or risk change in any area. This approach results in a life of mediocrity and hiding. The best way to build self-worth is to take risks and to succeed in an immediate goal. Then, goal by goal, we achieve and begin to realize that we're not failures. We are only failures when we quit or when we settle for mediocrity.

REFLECTION QUESTIONS

Describe an incident(s) in your childhood that affected your self-worth.

How does this incident(s) still affect you today?

If your answer to the previous incident was one that affected you negatively, what might you need to change to overcome that negative effect? If it was a positive incident, how can you continue to build on that good experience?

Do you struggle with believing that your issues are permanent—that they will never go away?

Below, list some issues you are dealing with, and then write a possible solution for one at least one of the problems.

Write a definition of yourself below, describing yourself to someone who doesn't know you.

Read Psalm 139:13–17. Based on what you read, write a definition of yourself as if God were describing you to another person.

REFLECTIONS

REFLECTIONS

REFLECTIONS

CHAPTER TWO

THE VARIOUS FACES OF LOW SELF-WORTH

*Low self-worth can manifest itself in many different ways—
addictions, codependency, anxiety, anger. It can damage
relationships and trap us in destructive patterns.
It holds us back from a life of freedom and health.*

One of the most common manifestations of low self-worth is what psychologists call the *fight or flight* response, which is an innate defense mechanism we use in the face of a threat or danger. There was a time when I frequently used this defense mechanism because I didn't have the ability to deal with conflict by working through it. My low self-worth caused me to move against any threatening situation with anger, or move away from it with shameful thoughts of not being perfect. I either attacked or ran. I even abandoned relationships with people who loved me because I had an erroneous fear they would end up hurting me.

Healthy confrontation wasn't a part of my life because I perceived it as criticism. I took it personally, thinking my whole life was a mistake, instead of isolating each incident. Relying on the fight or flight response has led to a trail of damaged relationships in my life.

SHAME

Shame is another face of low self-worth. It's one thing to be ashamed of the mistakes we've made, but it's another to be ashamed of *who we are*. Those dealing with low self-worth are usually bound with shame. Robert S. McGee writes in *The Search for Significance:* "When we base our self-worth on past failures, dissatisfaction with personal appearance, or bad habits, we often develop a . . . false belief: *I am what I am. I cannot change. I am hopeless.*"[1]

Most of us come out of our childhoods with a core sense of shame. We protect ourselves from a sense of overwhelming shame by creating a false self to protect those deep feelings of inadequacies and insecurities. Then we project that false self to others in order to gain approval and acceptance—but a level of fear remains. In my life, the greater the importance of the relationship, the more I would pretend and live out of my false self, which created an enormous amount of tension. I feared being discovered as a fraud.

In David Foster Wallace's short story, "Good Old Neon," his protagonist feels trapped in what he calls a "fraudulence paradox":

My whole life I've been a fraud. I'm not exaggerating. Pretty much all I've ever done all the time is try to create a certain impression of me in other people. Mostly to be liked or admired. It's a little more complicated than that, maybe. But when you come right down to it, it's to be liked, loved. Admired, approved of, applauded, whatever. You get the idea.

There was a basic logical paradox that I called the "fraudulence paradox" that I had discovered more or less on my own while taking a mathematical logic course in school. . . . The fraudulence paradox was that the more time and effort you put into trying to appear impressive or attractive to other people, the less impressive or attractive you felt inside—you were a fraud. And the more of a fraud you felt like, the harder you tried to convey an impressive or likable image of yourself so that other people wouldn't find out what a hollow, fraudulent person you really were.[2]

I've felt like the character in Wallace's short story most of my life. I told myself, *If they really knew you, they would not approve of you.* So I projected a fraudulent self in the hope of being accepted.

The danger of living as a fraudulent person is the failure to embrace intimacy in relationships. When we project a false self, we enter the relationship from the pretence of a lie. Intimacy can't exist without honesty.

In his book, *Healing the Shame That Binds You*, John Bradshaw writes,

What I discovered was that *shame as a healthy human emotion can be transformed into shame as a state of being. As a state of being shame takes over one's whole identity. To have shame as an identity is to believe that one's being is flawed, that one is defective as a human being. Once shame is transformed into an identity, it becomes toxic and dehumanizing.*

Toxic shame is unbearable and always necessitates a cover-up, a false self. Since one feels his true self is defective and flawed, one needs a false self that is not defective and flawed. *Once one becomes a false self, one ceases to exist psychologically.* To be a false self is to cease being an authentic human being.[3]

This is the great danger of a false self, which derives its energy from shame. Feelings of low self-worth and inadequacy can become a form of toxic shame. We take on a new identity and cease to be authentic, which makes us feel empty inside. We may have a hard time in relationships, because having a relationship with someone means we let them inside and let them get to know us. But if there's no one to know—other than the projected false self—our friends and loved ones will feel as if we never open up and allow them to love us. A person with a projected false self will hear people say, "You never let me know what's going on inside. You hold it all in. How can I love you when you won't let me?"

Others hit the wall we've built to protect ourselves from feeling shame, from feeling inadequate, from being rejected.

The great hope is that the people who love us will love us enough to tear down the wall. But we have to help them. No one is able to do all the work for us when it comes to tearing down the wall of shame. Ultimately, it comes down to a matter of trust. Will this person inflict shame or rejection? Of course, we can't predict the ultimate reaction when we expose our core identity. But if you'll examine your shame, you may discover that you're rejecting yourself by using a false self, confirming your inadequacy. The longer you live in the isolation of a false self, the more vulnerable you become to depression, addictions, and dysfunctional relationships. The catalyst to freedom of the bondage of low self-worth is the recognition of the lies you believe about yourself.

FEAR OF REJECTION

Fear of rejection often goes hand in hand with low self-worth because both relate to our performance. I'm very familiar with this fear in particular; it has been an issue at the core of my identity. For a long time, I felt I wasn't good enough, although I don't know where that message came from. It didn't come from my parents—they were very affirming and spoke positive words to me. Perhaps it came from comparing myself to others, or maybe from society's powerful messages, but I experienced terror at the thought of being rejected. I learned at an early age that performance could control what others thought of me.

Robert S. McGee writes, "Consciously or unconsciously, all of us have experienced this feeling that we must meet certain arbitrary standards to attain self-worth. Failure to do so threatens our security and significance. Such a threat, real or perceived, results in a fear of failure. At that point, we are accepting the false belief: *I must meet certain standards to feel good about myself.*"[4]

McGee calls this the "performance trap." One of the major epiphanies in my life happened when I realized that a deep feeling of inadequacy kept me in the performance trap. I felt I would be rejected for low performance or no performance, so I was always on alert. *Am I performing well? Will I be accepted for my performance?* And, of course, this fear doesn't go away entirely, because you're always judged by how well you do the next task. My freedom finally began when I realized the truth—that there were good things in me and there were bad things in me. No one is perfect all of the time. We must realize this if we ever hope to experience unconditional love.

ISOLATION

Another face of low self-worth is isolation. Those of us with low self-worth often isolate from other people and hide. We pull away and withdraw in relationships, because the deeper our fears of being rejected, the deeper our isolation. Often, we isolate ourselves with addictions. This is one of the great draws to pornography, especially on the internet. With pornography, we will never be rejected because we are escaping into fantasies. Anyone, even those who are married and live with a houseful of loved ones, can feel lonely and secretly hide in the isolation of addiction.

Isolation stems from the fear of being known, and thus being rejected. Nothing good ever comes from isolation—but don't confuse isolation with solitude. Seeking solitude, especially with God and self, is a very healthy thing. We need times of contemplation and prayer and meditation. We *need* solitude. Isolation is *not* solitude. Isolation is a withdrawal from life, an escape from our fears and shame.

The opposite of isolation is intimacy. Intimacy is being vulnerable and honest, making myself known. I am connecting with other human beings. In isolation, I don't want to be known by other human beings. I don't want to connect or be honest.

Isolation leads to even deeper feelings of low self-worth. Coming out of isolation, into the light, is one of the most important keys to a person's emotional healing. Surround yourself with encouraging and supportive people, and it will foster a healing environment. The benefit of being in a group—like the ones we sponsor at Restore Ministries—is learning universality, learning that we are not alone. We realize other people have struggled in much the same way as we have, which encourages us to come out of isolation. We find freedom and healing in the light. But when we retreat into the darkness and hide in a place of secrecy, we find ourselves slipping back into bondage. C. S. Lewis writes,

> I would much rather say that every time you make a choice you are turning the central part of you . . . into something a little different from what it was before. And taking your life as a whole, with all your innumerable choices, all your life long you are slowly turning this central thing either into a heavenly creature or into a hellish creature: either into a creature that is in harmony with God, and with creatures, and with itself, or else into one that is in a state of war and hatred with God, and with its fellow creatures, and with itself.[5]

Sharing intimacy in our relationships is how we choose to be heavenly creatures. This is the great joy of intimacy: *I am no longer alone. I'm connected to another human being with all of my good parts and my bad. I can truly be who I am and who God created me to be.* But when we choose to isolate and withdraw, we are choosing a state of disharmony. We are losing touch with our central identity.

Melissa's Story

Melissa got saved when she was fourteen. She began to feel guilt that even with Christ's help her behavior couldn't be controlled. "I embraced the unhealthy belief that the Christian thing to do was to always put myself last. That was being humble, what God expected of me. It became such a habit that I no longer knew how to speak up for myself. I didn't know how to say what I wanted; I didn't even know what I wanted.

"I didn't have close friends, because I feared intimacy. I knew that if I let my guard down, I would have reveal parts of myself that I wanted to remain secret. I was crippled by shame."

Melissa enjoyed college, though the excitement and distraction wasn't enough to keep her out of the low places. "During my sophomore year, I decided to take control of my weight. I decided to eat only once a day and did that for several months. I lost a lot of weight rapidly—about seventy-five pounds by the end of the year—and I thought that was great. I was happy. Then I hit another low that started several years—which I'm just starting to come out of—of ups and downs in my weight and emotions. I'd lose eighty pounds, then gain forty, or lose twenty, then gain thirty.

"When I met Adam, I still felt very low about myself, but I started trying to do things for him. I wanted to lose weight *for him*. I wanted to take care *of him*. And it was always *him*. I didn't know how to tell him what I needed, because I didn't know what I needed from him."

Their relationship deepened quickly, and Melissa knew Adam was the man she would marry. But the low points continued to come and go as their wedding plans and early marriage brought new stresses.

SELF-REJECTION

Each of us tends to have an inner voice that speaks to us. You might call it your conscience. But I believe we can also develop a neurotic inner critic that constantly disapproves of every move we make. This harsh inner critic cultivates low self-worth. When our self-worth is low, we are operating from a place of inadequacy. One of the most painful responses from this inner critic is rejection. It's hard to live with ourselves if we reject our core identity. If I reject myself, then—in a sense—I'm rejecting my life. And that is difficult to deal with since I am the one person I must live with.

If my core identity is marked by self-rejection, I will enter into relationships needing approval to feel good about myself. Affirmation from others is vital, but it can cripple our relationships if we are needy, if we are always seeking approval from others. This is usually where codependency comes in: I become dependent on you to make me feel good about myself.

When I reject myself, I am denying the love God has for me. If I don't believe God loves me, then I find it difficult to love others. Jesus said, "Love your neighbor as yourself" (Matt. 22:39 NIV). We cannot give away what we do not have. The inner belief that we're good, loveable, and worthy of hopes and dreams, is how we discover freedom—freedom to be who we are at the core. Each of us is in charge of how we love ourselves, and we cannot do it apart from God.

There are so many forces that can lead us to a place of self-rejection—drugs, alcohol, sexual addictions, loneliness, emptiness. As long as we seek an answer outside of ourselves and without God, we will be susceptible to the forces mentioned above.

And it's worth mentioning that I'm not talking about self-centeredness, but self-worth. There's a huge difference. Selfish people cannot love others because they are too busy loving themselves. Aaron Beck, in his book *Prisoners of Hate,* writes: "We all have the tendency to perceive ourselves as the lead actor of a play and to judge other people's behavior exclusively in reference to ourselves. We take the role of the protagonist and the other players are our supporters or antagonists. The motivations and actions of the other players revolve around us in some way."[6] This is the danger of self-centeredness. But the person who loves himself and is comfortable in his own skin will be able to love others and help support them.

DISHONESTY

Another face of low self-worth is dishonesty. A person that has positive self-worth is generally an honest person. It's almost as if the ability to be honest is a byproduct of a healthy self-worth. Why? Because it's easier to be truthful when you are not afraid of being rejected. But for those of us who have low self-worth, there is a tendency to be dishonest, especially in matters of the heart. We are living from a dishonest place, a place of deceit. We're afraid to admit our mistakes because we fear rejection. In his book *Power to Choose*, Mike O'Neil says that we are only as sick as our secrets. I believe that is true.

At Restore, we've noticed that people are able to experience true intimacy in our safe, small recovery groups. We work through the twelve steps and begin to take a personal inventory. Then participants confess their mistakes to other people and to God. For many of us, it is the first time we are honest about ourselves. C. S. Lewis said, "God can show Himself as He really is only to real (people). And that means not simply to (people) who are individually good, but to (people) who are united together in a body, loving one another, helping one another, showing Him to one another. For that is what God meant humanity to be like; like players in one band, or organs in one body."[7]

When group members tell the truth about what they're going through and what is going on in their hearts, it develops intimacy and fosters self-worth. When we lie and live in deceit and dishonesty, it magnifies feelings of low self-worth. We must extinguish dishonesty before it sets the whole soul ablaze with low self-worth.

REFLECTION QUESTIONS

Describe your ideal self. Who would you be if nothing were holding you back?

What would you have to change about yourself in order to be this ideal person?

What feelings come to mind as you look at your answers to the previous two questions?

List some of the good qualities that you believe you possess.

List some of the bad qualities that you possess.

What would it mean for you to be able to accept your whole self—both the good and the bad?

REFLECTIONS

REFLECTIONS

REFLECTIONS

CHAPTER 3

OVERCOMING LOW SELF-WORTH BY DISCOVERING OUR PASSIONS

FedEx CEO and founder Fred Smith first developed the idea for an innovative airfreight company while he was a student at Yale University. His professor was less than impressed. The paper Smith submitted, outlining the concept, earned him a C. Thirty years later, FedEx is the world's largest express transportation company with 128,000 employees and more than seven billion dollars in capital. This shortsighted professor didn't take into account Smith's persistence, and Smith simply refused to give up. He was also highly successful at recruiting others to his vision—people wanted to be a part of Smith's plans! In the early years, his pilots often refueled company jets with their own money. Sometimes they sat on paychecks for months to help keep the company afloat. They believed in Smith, but they also caught the vision of the company.

The way to overcome low self-worth is to have a vision. The vision can be as simple as being employee of the month or as challenging as starting a company like FedEx. But the person who never finds a vision to live by will soon settle into a life of chronic low self-worth. Without a vision or a purpose, our lives tend to feel empty and hopeless.

We tend to have a low level of chronic depression and live in an apathetic mindset. We lower our expectations for life and see ourselves as incapable, inferior, flawed, and inadequate. Pessimism permeates our lives.

Dr. Harry Emerson Fosdick once said fatalism is one of the most comfortable moods in which a person can live. I can relate to this because, in the past, I've always had the feeling I wouldn't be able to succeed. When I experienced an ambitious desire for something, I would immediately hear the inner critic tell me I couldn't do it. Heeding that voice became a protective way for me to live. I believed if I could exist in a state of low expectations, then I wouldn't feel like a failure. So I stopped taking risks and settled on feeling miserable. I felt nothing good would come of my life. I stalemated. My life hit a wall, and I stopped believing in the possibility that I could be happy. Once we become hopeless, we stop living from a place of dreams and vision. In the Bible, it says, "Where there is no vision, the people perish."[1]

Abraham Lincoln struggled with depression and fatalism. He once said, "I am now the most miserable man living. If what I feel were equally distributed to the whole human family, there would not be one cheerful face on earth." Even though Lincoln felt this way, he didn't allow it to immobilize him. He moved toward a vision of one day becoming president. Fosdick said about Lincoln, "The mirrors of his mind turned more and more to windows. His devotion to a cause greater than himself transformed what he had learned in his long struggle with himself into insight, understanding, sympathy, humor, wisdom."[2]

LIVING WITH A PASSION

One of the most common symptoms of low self-worth is hopelessness. We stop dreaming. We stop fostering creativity. We stop taking risks. The loss of our dreams paralyzes us. We sit around and let life pass us by. Then, at the end of our lives, we realize we never fully lived.

In 1904, William Borden—the heir to the Borden Dairy fortune—graduated from high school in Chicago. His family gave him a cruise around the world as a graduation gift. As he traveled around the world, he wrote several letters home. As his trip progressed, the letters began to change. He saw the hurts and the needs in the world, and it caused him to have compassion. In one letter he wrote,

Mom,
I believe God is calling me to be a missionary.

Another letter said,

I'm sure God is calling me. I'm going to prepare and give my life to the mission field.

This was not what the family had hoped for him, the oldest and most gifted son in the family. But when he got home from his trip, William went to college for four years and then to a theological seminary for three. He spent *seven years* preparing for the mission field. While he was in school, he gave away his part of the family inheritance because he wanted to be totally dependent upon God. After giving away his mass of wealth, he opened to the back flyleaf of his Bible and wrote two words, "No reserves."

Around William's last year in seminary, his father became sick. The family wanted William to remain at home and take over the family business, because he was the oldest and the only capable one in the family. Their livelihood depended upon the business. They offered him whatever salary he wanted and any car he wanted. They even offered to give him his father's office.

William looked at them and said, "No, my life is committed now."

Then he opened up to the back flyleaf of his Bible and wrote two more words, "No retreats."

After seven years of schooling, he was ready for the mission field. He left for China, because he felt God was calling him to a group of Muslims there. He stopped in Egypt for a respite, and contracted cerebral meningitis. He was dead within a month. William had prepared for seven years for the mission field, but never made it. He never realized his dream. It went unfulfilled.

At some point after William's death, his family opened to the back flyleaf of his Bible and not only did they find those other words he had written—"No reserves" and "No retreats"—but they also found two more words he'd written before his death—"No regrets."[3]

The startling thing about William Borden's life is his untimely death. It's hard to hear about unfulfilled dreams. But we envy a person who lives with passion as William Borden did, because most of us have settled for jobs and careers that are unfulfilling. We don't have a clue what we want to do with our lives. But the answer to an empty life is to discover vision, because vision gives us purpose, and purpose produces passion. Otherwise, life becomes boring and lethargic. This is the chronic, low-level depression so many of us live in. We give up on our dreams and settle, then we become miserable. It's a kind of slow death.

Melissa's Story

Melissa has discovered her own passions during her recovery—and found that her "passions" of yesterday were not truly passions. She had some fun, was an excellent student, and played a mean oboe. But these were not passions for her. She feared true passion, much as she feared life itself. "I was afraid to take risks, afraid to experience anything. I knew that those new things could bring me hurt, and I was already hurting enough! But now, my passion is just in living life to its fullest. It's okay if I take risks, if I fail. I want to make a difference. I know that there will be setbacks, and there will be times when I doubt things will work out for the best. But I know it's all a part of God's plan. I'm passionate about being a tool for God! I have a passion to help kids that have had similar experiences to me. My heart aches for them. I see myself as that little girl on the playground who has no one to play with, the little girl with duct tape on her shoes because the soles are coming off. I know what it's like; I feel that hurt. I want God to use me to reach out to those kids. I believe that's why I've gone through what I have. That's why I'm here."

OVERCOMING TEDIUM

Low-grade chronic depression can produce an overarching feeling of tedium in our lives. When nothing seems to inspire us, we don't respect our lives enough to live every day to the fullest. We mope along like Frank Wheeler in the novel *Revolutionary Road*. Frank works a boring job at Knox Business Machines on the fifteenth floor of the Knox Building. He believes the great advantage of a place like Knox is that you can turn off your mind every morning at nine, leave it off all day, and nobody knows the difference. This existence has taught him new ways of spacing out the hours of the day—almost time to go down for coffee; almost time to go out for lunch; almost time to go home.[4] The danger of Frank Wheeler's life is how he throws away chunks of time each day, enduring life instead of living it to the fullest.

Most of us live like Frank Wheeler. We're stuck in jobs that don't inspire passion, because we've convinced ourselves that life is a matter of paying the bills and work is something that we have to survive each day. But the reality is that we have a limited amount of time on earth; the mortality rate is 100 percent. Sadly, most of us never live to the fullest until we find out we are going to die. Only then do we seriously begin to think about doing something that will live on after our death.

REGAINING INTEGRITY

Integrity is a powerful principle. One of the greatest gifts of having positive self-worth is that we have a sense of integrity and discover the strength to be our authentic selves. We believe in ourselves. We say what we mean and live consistently within our values. Integrity is being honest with self. *Am I happy? Do I feel fulfilled?* Often we convince ourselves that we are happy and fulfilled by settling for less than our passions and purpose. We pretend to be professional when we're miserable. We work to win approval because we believe this is what society expects from us. We try to be perfect parents, perfect employees, even perfect Christians. And when we don't measure up to perfection, we fake it. We act as fake professionals in a fake professional world, and it erodes our integrity. But instead of changing the state of our existence, we become resentful and bitter for having to live this way.

When God started to rebuild my self-worth, I began to tell the truth. I had completely lost my integrity during my addictive years. I couldn't face life when I woke up in the morning. I was anxious about having to hold up the mask. But the more I turned away from the false life I once led, a sense of integrity returned.

OVERCOMING PROCRASTINATION

Procrastination is another cause of low self-worth, because it causes us to postpone positive change. Whereas denial is a rejection of the truth, procrastination accepts the truth but delays the action it takes to correct the problem, creating a habitual pattern. Most procrastinators believe in an elusive "six months out" plan, saying, "I'm going to do something about this, but let's just give it six more months to see what happens." We procrastinate because we don't want to confront the truth about ourselves. We don't want to walk down the difficult path, do the hard work, or endure the pain and discomfort that sometimes comes with being honest with ourselves.

Procrastination also thrives on fear. When we fear that what we think about ourselves is true, we feel inadequate to change. Once this fear sets in, we end up living in a place of bleakness. Everything seems empty because we've pushed life "six months out" into the future. The present has no real significance. Our energy becomes low, and the little things in our daily lives become exhausting. Then we live to procrastinate. We feel overwhelmed and put off things of importance. Project deadlines come and go. Sometimes we can't even get started—we don't feel up to the task. We let our eating get out of control, while telling ourselves we'll do something about it tomorrow. But we never do.

If you look up procrastination in the dictionary, you might find my picture next to this word. I was once the king of procrastination. I tended to put off anything that was going to take thought and effort because I was afraid of failure. I would also procrastinate if confrontation was involved. If I needed to talk to someone and clear things up, I would avoid that person at all costs. Somehow I felt he or she would discover my inadequacies and reject me. It all came down to those core feelings of not being good enough—feelings that left me cowering in fear. Every time I put off confrontation, it would end up brewing into anger, making things worse. Or, I'd live with anxiety, anticipating the worst possible scenario. If I'd had the worth and confidence to confront the situation in the beginning, I would have spared myself much worry. The person I was in conflict with would usually end up saying, "Scott, we should have had this conversation a long time ago."

When we struggle with low self-esteem, we tend to look into the future and believe that the outcome will be negative. So we procrastinate to avoid what we see as a bleak outcome. Procrastination is a way to retreat. When a person begins to live a life of vision, and is focused on something positive, he or she begins to feel passionate about moving forward. Where there is passion, there is courage—courage to endure though obstacles to reach an important goal.

Procrastination is fear-based. Passion and vision are faith-based. People who have a perspective of healthy self-worth aren't afraid to take some risks, because they know that if they fail, they can grow, adapt, make adjustments, and move on. They keep trying. Why? Because there is nothing wrong with failure. There is only one ultimate failure, and that is to quit trying.

REFLECTION QUESTIONS

Fosdick believed Lincoln was able to turn from his inward self-loathing by looking to causes greater than himself. Do you have a cause greater than yourself? Have you ever wanted to start a business, a family, a career in politics, or volunteer for a non-profit organization, but felt unworthy of the vision? Explain.

What does *integrity* mean to you?

Do you feel you have integrity? Do you ever feel that you've compromised your integrity? What do you think caused you to do that?

Are you procrastinating in some area of your life? Why do you think you are procrastinating?

What is one way that you can move forward in this area of your life, instead of continuing to procrastinate?

REFLECTIONS

REFLECTIONS

CHAPTER 4

FOUNDATIONS FOR POSITIVE SELF-WORTH

A farmer looked out his window one day and saw several young men stealing watermelons from his field. He pulled out his gun and fired over the thieves heads once or twice to scare them. They scattered, each running in his own direction.

Later, when the young men had gathered, one said, "Did you hear those bullets?"

Another replied, "I heard them twice: once when they passed me and once when I passed them!"

Fear is a powerful feeling that directs our behavior. It can make us run and tremble. It can even cause us to have unsubstantiated thoughts about our safety. When we make decisions based solely on fear, we stop taking risks. We become stagnant and stop growing. We are unable to step into the life God wants for us because we don't believe it is possible.

So often we perceive ourselves as being inferior and incapable of standing up to the so-called giants in our lives. Low self-worth makes everyone else loom larger than they really are. When we believe other people are better and stronger, we are comparing ourselves unjustly. We defeat ourselves before we even start. But with God, all things are possible. God created us with specific gifts and talents to work out His purpose through our lives. But we limit ourselves when we view our abilities apart from God.

Melissa's Story

Melissa walked into a YMCA one day and saw posters for Restore Ministries. She signed up and contacted a counselor. "I didn't know what else to do. I knew I was hitting these walls . . . [but] I always thought I could fix things alone. I realized that I'd need some extra help. So I got in with Restore, and I just fell to pieces.

"It was such a totally different experience to have somebody there that I could be vulnerable with and who wouldn't take advantage of that. People were there to help me and wouldn't give advice based on what they thought I should do, but based on what the Bible says—based on knowledge of the truths of God. It was so healing to me."

Melissa is finding that with her new passions, she's experiencing the joy of new goals—goals that are hers and no one else's. "I've always wanted to finish a degree. I was a good student in school, and even when I was a little kid, I always wanted to graduate from college. When I was in college, I went through several low periods, so I decided to take a break. And I needed to, because I was really there to please my parents. It was my best plan to try to get them involved in my life. But they never came to visit me, and that plan fell through. I decided to move, to take a break. Then fear set in: *What if I don't have what it takes to finish school?* I got to a point where I was so afraid that I didn't want to go back. In order for this dream to come true, I had to be ready to do it simply because I wanted to—not for anyone else."

DEFINE YOURSELF

Suppose that during the past week a young wife gave birth to her first baby. Now suppose that as she held her new baby in her arms and was enjoying the pleasure of motherhood, someone came up to her and said, "How much do you want for the child?" Of course she would be horrified at the suggestion that her precious baby was for sale. But the stranger is persistent and offers ten thousand dollars, then a hundred thousand, and finally one million dollars. The offers are in vain because the mother will simply press the baby closer to her heart and reply, "My baby is worth more to me than the entire world."

Of course, if she didn't say that, we would question whether she had the proper attitude for motherhood. But *why* does she say it? Because she looks forward to a thousand dirty diapers, sleepless nights with a sick child, and the costs of raising that child? Because the child will bring her fame and fortune? Of course not. Rather, she has chosen to value this tiny person, to deem the small one to be of worth, because it is *hers.* Such worth resides in the very identity of a person, not in his or her perform-ance. And such worth, based on the image of God in all of us, must be the basis of our concept of ourselves, too, if our self-portrait is to be durable and worthwhile.[1]

Our self-worth resides in our identity. Defining ourselves from a nega-tive perspective is so easy to do in this world. We live in a harsh, cynical, critical society where comparison is inevitable: *This one is the pretty one. That one is the dumb one.* For those with low self-worth, it's more natural to dwell on the negative—to define ourselves as worthless, rather than con-centrate on our positive aspects. Do you realize that humans may very well be the only living creatures that define themselves? Animals don't judge one another or critique themselves all day. As far as we know, one cat doesn't call another cat a "fat cat." Nor does a slow cheetah see himself as flawed. Humans define themselves physically, spiritually, and men-tally. We label ourselves and create negative self-talk. It's deeply engrained in our society to do so.

We need to be careful of allowing negative self-talk to permeate our careers and relationships. These toxic thoughts have the power to limit us, causing us to miss the joy of being loved, or hindering us from reaching our full potentials. Dr. Gerald May, a psychiatrist and spiritual counselor, writes in his book *Addiction and Grace*:

> First, although God calls us all toward a more perfect life, we cannot personally achieve the state of perfection. We can and should do our very best to move in that direction, struggling with every resource we have, but we must also accept the reality of our incompleteness. Second, we need to recognize that the incompleteness within us, our personal insufficiency, does not make us unacceptable in God's eyes. Far from it; our incompleteness is the empty side of our longing for God and for love. It is what draws us toward God and one another. If we do not fill our minds with guilt and self-recriminations, we will recognize our incompleteness as a kind of spaciousness into which we can welcome the flow of grace. We can think of our inadequacies as terrible defects, if we want, and hate ourselves. But we can also think of them affirmatively, as doorways through which the power of grace can enter our lives. Then we may begin to appreciate our inherent, God given lovableness.[2]

CREATED TO SERVE

One person who understood what Dr. Gerald May was talking about was Mother Teresa. She lived a life of service. She was anything but self-consumed, as evidenced in her life's work. This diminutive woman wasn't very attractive by the world's standards, but she never seemed to worry about her appearance. She didn't have any amazing physical talents, only an amazing heart for God and for people. She loved caring for the "least of these" and spent her entire life serving them. She didn't focus on herself first; she focused on serving and loving God. C. S. Lewis once said that every Christian would agree that a person's spiritual health is exactly proportional to his love for God.[3]

The key to developing a healthy sense of self-worth is to realize we are created to serve, to give our lives for a cause greater than ourselves. It is in giving that we receive God's best. We need to believe who God says we are. We must know that we are unconditionally loved and created by Him to give, to share, and to be a blessing to others. That purpose shifts the focus off of ourselves. I tell people in group sessions that if the most work they put into recovery is to merely sit in their chairs and listen, then they are focusing on self. But if they show up early, help set up chairs before our meeting, or help brew coffee, they will begin to stop thinking of themselves. Small acts of kindness make a big impact on our self-worth.

LEARN TO SERVE

If we can learn to give something from our lives to others without needing something in return—no strings attached—then we have a genuine kindness in our heart for others. When we begin to see people in recovery give unconditionally, their hearts tend to overflow. Without even thinking, they begin to set up chairs, fix coffee, and greet people. They begin to embrace servanthood, to give away what has been given to them. And, for the first time in a long while, they feel good about themselves.

By a coincidence of circumstances one day, I helped a blind man sit down in a chair. A few days later at a luncheon, I helped a handicapped man get his wheelchair unstuck, and he thanked me. Then, sometime later, I helped a young girl with shriveled hands tie her shoes, so she could get on her way. Those small acts of kindness made me feel good about being me. I didn't get anything in return for those acts, but I believe they made God smile. He created me to serve—to care for others who can't care for themselves.

As a young man, James L. Kraft, founder of Kraft Foods, wanted to be the most famous manufacturer and salesman of cheese in the world. He planned to become rich and famous by making and selling cheese, beginning as a young fellow with a little buggy pulled by a pony named Paddy. After making his cheese, he would load his wagon and he and Paddy would drive down the streets of Chicago to sell it. As months passed, young Kraft began to despair because he was not making any money, in spite of his long hours and hard work.

One day he pulled his pony to a stop and began to talk to him. He said, "Paddy, there is something wrong. We are not doing it right. I am afraid we have things turned around and our priorities are not where they ought to be. Maybe we ought to serve God and place Him first in our lives." Kraft then drove home and made a covenant that for the rest of his life he would serve God first and then work as God directed.

KEEP DREAMING

In the Bible, God says that without a vision, we perish. Let's think about that from the perspective of self-esteem. Having a vision means we have a passionate pursuit that gives meaning to our lives. It makes us feel alive. We don't need drugs, food, alcohol, obsessions, or relationships to give our life meaning. It's an intrinsic feeling of well-being. It's what Mother Teresa meant when she said, "It is not the magnitude of our actions but the amount of love that is put into them that matters."

In the movie *Dreamer*, Ben Crane (Kurt Russell) believes that a severely injured racehorse deserves another chance. He and his daughter Cale (Dakota Fanning) adopt the horse, saving it from its demise. The arrival of the mare to the Crane's farm provides an opportunity for father and daughter to reconstruct their fractured relationship. After Cale writes an essay for a school assignment, her father must come to class and read it. Cale has written about how she hopes this horse will heal her father's broken heart and solve their family struggles. Reading the essay, Ben is moved by Cale's dream, but he still doesn't believe the horse will race again. He knows it's a long shot. And in one scene, Ben tells his wife that Cale's dream is a pipedream that will soon crush her. But Ben's wife says, "So what! You have forgotten how to dream! Let her have her dream. Let it carry her as far as it can!"

Let your dreams carry you as far as they can. We are created to dream. It's what makes me get up in the morning, ready to face life with passion. I let it carry me as far as I can! Dreams can help build our self-esteem when we actually go for them. Cale's dream for the horse and for her family wasn't about how much money they could make. It wasn't about ego and glory. It was a simple dream about how this horse could give her father his heart back. So today, start thinking about your dream and let it carry you as far as it can.

EMBRACE HUMILITY

Television newsman Tom Brokaw was wandering through Bloomingdale's in New York City one day, shortly after he was promoted to co-host of *Today*. After years of working, first in Omaha and then for NBC in Los Angeles and Washington, he was feeling good about himself and his new job. As he walked through the store, he noticed a man watching him closely. The man kept staring at him and finally, when the man approached, Brokaw was sure he was about to reap the first fruits of being a New York television celebrity.

The man pointed his finger and said, "Tom Brokaw, right?"

"Right," said Brokaw.

"You used to do the morning news on KMTV in Omaha, right?"

"That's right," said Brokaw, getting set for the accolades to follow.

"I knew it the minute I saw spotted you," the man said. Then he paused and added, "Whatever happened to you?"[4]

We may not be television newsmen, but all of us have thought better of ourselves than we really are. There's nothing wrong with having a healthy desire for love and admiration. It's built into who we are. So celebrate yourself, but don't let your ego get the best of you.

Psalm 51:17 says that God loves a broken and contrite (remorseful) heart. Now, when we think about the kind of heart God loves, a broken and contrite heart is probably not at the top of our lists. We expect God to love a joyful heart or a thankful heart—but a broken and contrite heart? The preacher Charles Haddon Spurgeon once said that people despise those who are disgraceful, but the Lord doesn't see as we do. He despises what people esteem and values what they despise. That's what Jesus does when he enters our lives—turns our world upside down, readjusting our values.

Humility is fertile soil for God to build self-worth through our service to Him. When we come to the end of ourselves, we become fertile soil for Jeremiah 29:11 to be planted in our heart—"For I know the thoughts that I think toward you, says the LORD, thoughts of peace and not of evil, to give you a future and a hope" (NKJV). God has a plan for my life. And when I believe that God has a plan for me, I am filled with hope because *God* is doing something good in me. It's not all up to me. In Romans 7:18 the apostle Paul said, "I know that nothing good lives in me, that is, in my sinful nature. For I have the desire to do what is good, but I cannot carry it out" (NIV). The good I can do comes from a power greater than my own. When we rest in God's power over our lives, we are free to embrace our own dignity and self-worth.

REFLECTION QUESTIONS

Have you ever limited yourself in some area because you feared you would fail? Give an example.

Missionary William Carey once said, "Expect great things from God, attempt great things for God." Do you believe you can expect great things from God? Why or why not?

Mark an X on the scale below indicating how loveable you see yourself.

1	2	3	4	5	6	7	8	9	10

Very Unlovable   Somewhat Lovable   Very Lovable

If you indicated that you see yourself as unlovable or even somewhat unlovable, what can you do to change this feeling?

If you could ask Mother Teresa any question, what would you ask and why?

Mother Teresa once said that she was a "little pencil in the hand of a writing God who is sending a love letter to the world." If your life is a little pencil in the hand of a writing God, what is the message of your letter to the world?

Would you say that your priorities are in order? Make a list of your top five priorities below.

REFLECTIONS

REFLECTIONS

REFLECTIONS

CHAPTER 5

THE IMPORTANCE OF PERSPECTIVE

An optimist invited a pessimist to go duck hunting. The optimist wanted to show off his new registered hunting dog that could do things no other dog could.

The pessimist looked at the dog and said, "Looks like a mutt to me."

At that moment, a flock of ducks flew over. The optimist shot one of the ducks and it fell into the middle of the lake. He snapped his fingers and the dog ran across the top of the water, picked up the duck, and ran back across the water to the hunters. The optimist took the duck from the dog's mouth, turned to the pessimist, and said, "What do you think of my dog now?"

The pessimist replied, "Dumb dog—can't even swim."

Perspective can mean everything. If we choose to be negative, will we view everything in a negative light. In the same respect, a positive perspective can help build self-worth. When we stop believing in the possibility that things can change, we become hopeless pessimists. We are unable to feel a sense of self-satisfaction, merely surviving on the fear of failure. This leaves us waiting for the next bad thing to happen.

In Judges 13, an angel came to Manoah and his wife, and told them they would have a son named Samson. Manoah and his wife offered a sacrifice to God:

> And the LORD did an amazing thing while Manoah and his wife watched: As the flame blazed up from the altar toward heaven, the angel of the LORD ascended in the flame. Seeing this, Manoah and his wife fell with their faces to the ground. When the angel of the LORD did not show himself again to Manoah and his wife, Manoah realized that it was the angel of the LORD.
>
> "We are doomed to die!" he said to his wife. "We have seen God!"
>
> But his wife answered, "If the LORD had meant to kill us, he would not have accepted a burnt offering and grain offering from our hands, nor shown us all these things or now told us this." (Judg. 13:19–23 NIV)

Manoah was afraid, but his wife put a positive spin on things for him. She used logic and common sense. She said in essence, "Manoah, you're being unrealistic." And it was true.

Sometimes we are like Manoah. We fail to see God at work in a positive way in our lives. We allow our fear and negativity to disregard the promise Jesus made to us that He will never leave us or forsake us.

SEEING TRUTH IN OUR PERSPECTIVES

After a motorist was in a collision, people on the scene pulled the unconscious man from his car and carried him to a nearby Shell station. As he regained consciousness, he opened his eyes and began struggling violently. No one understood why, so they subdued him and transported him to a nearby hospital. Sometime later, he explained why he'd struggled to get away from his rescuers: at the Shell station, he awoke and looked around, and what he saw frightened him—someone was standing in front of the S on the sign.

Sometimes what we see doesn't line up with the truth. We can easily believe wrong things about ourselves. The ability to recognize truth is essential for healthy self-worth. If we can recognize truth, we can know when our inner critic or someone else distorts it. We are able to say, "They aren't thinking straight." Arthur Freeman and Rose DeWolf write in *Woulda, Coulda, Shoulda:* "Analyzing what you are thinking lies at the core of cognitive therapy, because how we think affects how we feel and how we behave. . . . [We] have simply allowed the situation [we] face to get the better of [our] common sense."[1]

We can overcome distortion in reality by using common sense. This is what Manoah's wife did. She reasoned. She thought things through. Maybe all that your situation requires is for you to think things through. Are you in a relationship with someone because you think that he or she is the only one you will ever find? Have you distorted the truth because you are really staving off feelings of loneliness? Relationships based on distortion of reality tend to have an "ah ha!" moment when it all becomes clear—that moment when we say, "How could I have been so stupid not to see this?"

When dealing with any issue, put it through the litmus test of common sense: Are your feelings rational? Do they add up and make good sense? Are you deceiving yourself for thinking like this?

OVERGENERALIZATION

Overgeneralization means taking a single event and generalizing the outcome to all events. When we overgeneralize, we don't feel safe. There's always the threat that a past event will happen again. A great biblical example of overgeneralization occurred when the children of Israel sent spies into the promised land. When the spies returned and reported what they saw to Moses, the consensus seemed divided. Some thought the land couldn't be taken from Israel's enemies, while others wanted to attack. "Caleb silenced the people before Moses and said, 'We should go up and take possession of the land, for we can certainly do it.' But the men who had gone up with him said, 'We can't attack those people; they are stronger than we are'" (Num. 13:30–31 NIV).

The doubting spies used overgeneralization to describe the strength of their enemies. Without even going into battle, they defeated themselves. We should never set limits on what we can accomplish by using overgeneralization. Sure, the odds were against the children of Israel if they discounted God's role in their situation. But isn't that the hope we still maintain—that God can make up for the gaps in our human strength? Jesus said, "With man this is impossible, but with God all things are possible" (Matt. 19:26 NIV). The odds may be against you, but you'll never know what you're capable of with God's power if you don't try. Sure, it's good to use common sense, but also realize that there's a greater power. God can make things happen.

CATASTROPHIZING

Catastrophizing is making a mountain out of a molehill. To catastrophize is to magnify our struggles, much like Gideon did when he was hiding from the battle. The angel of the Lord came to him and said, "The Lord is with you, you mighty man of valor!" (Judg, 6:12 NKJV). But Gideon certainly didn't feel like a man of valor. If he had felt like a mighty warrior, then he wouldn't have been hiding out. He even replied, "If the Lord is with us, why then has all this happened to us?" (v.13). Gideon had fallen into the trap of catastrophizing. He'd evidently been stewing about why God wasn't acting on Israel's behalf. He expected God to act when God wanted Gideon to take action. God wanted Gideon to get outside of his rumination and stop mulling over the negative aspects of the situation. To do this, Gideon would have to replace his negative, catastrophic thoughts with positive, overcoming ones.

Change is a program of replacement. As we practice new self-dialogue and affirmations and begin to visualize the new people we want to become, these new ways take root and replace old behaviors. It's like digging up a weed-laden garden. We uproot the old and make way for the new. We plant new seeds, water them, and give them time to grow and establish roots. It takes time, patience, and vigilant effort. This is what Gideon eventually did. He became a mighty warrior and defeated Israel's enemies.

MINIMIZING

Minimizing occurs when we downplay our responsibility in a decision, when that decision turns out to be wrong. We build self-worth by owning our mistakes, and then by correcting them in the future. Consider the boy who broke the glass of a streetlamp. He went home and asked his father what he should do. "Do?" exclaimed his father, "Why, we must report it and ask what you must pay, then go and settle it."

This practical way of dealing with the matter was not what the boy had in mind, and he whimpered, "I—I—thought all I had to do was ask God to forgive me."

The boy was trying to minimize his responsibility.

When we minimize our responsibility we never fully own up to our mistakes. We justify our actions, and justification weakens our self-worth. We may be ashamed that we lack the strength to do the right thing, and we're afraid of being seen as weak, so we try to minimize.

COMPARATIVE THINKING

When we compare ourselves to others and feel that we don't measure up, it tears away at our self-worth. The apostle Paul said, "For we dare not class ourselves or compare ourselves with those who commend themselves. But they, measuring themselves by themselves, and comparing themselves among themselves, are not wise" (2 Cor. 10:12 NKJV).

When we look around at other people who seem to be better than us, it tends to bring us down. It devalues us. We feel cheated. Then we conclude that we must have a fatal flaw, which lowers our self-worth.

Melissa's Story

Melissa has been given the gift of new perspective: "I found my voice; I learned to speak up for myself. I learned that I am not a horrible person because I can't stop eating sometimes when I am upset.

"We had this unspoken rule in my house that you weren't supposed to cry, you weren't supposed to talk back, you weren't supposed to *feel*, basically—and if you did you got in big trouble for it. I learned the truth that emotions are God-given, that they should be embraced and felt. God created us to be emotional people. 'Emotional' used to be derogatory to me, but I now see emotion in a different light.

"If I was at my own funeral, and I was able to watch my spouse and my kids and friends talk about me, I would want them to say that I didn't quit. That I was sometimes weak, but I found my strength through God. That I wasn't perfect, but I strove to be the best that I could. I'd ultimately want them to understand, above all things, how much I loved them, and how much I loved experiencing life with them. I'd want them to talk about the joy of God that they saw in me.

"I'd want them to talk about what God has done—not what I have done, but what God has done."

AFFIRMING SELF-WORTH

A big part of what we do at Restore Ministries is affirm self-worth. In our small group sessions, we actually structure time to show appreciation whenever a person shares something about his or her life. We acknowledge courage and growth. It's something we practice with each other because for some, it's the only place they receive positive messages about who they are. Often when a person is making a life change, such as recovering from an addictive behavior, there will be slips and relapses. It is a struggle to stay on the path of recovery. If there is just one thing that a recovering addict does well in a day, he or she needs to affirm and take credit for that accomplishment.

It is so important that we speak positive messages of self-worth into our lives if we hope to make a permanent change. At the end of our group sessions at Restore Ministries, we have a little activity where we put each individual in a chair in the middle of the group. We call out positive affirmations about who God has created this person to be, who they are becoming, and how we see them in a positive way. Every time we do this, we are amazed at the reaction and response of the person in the middle. To hear from fellow trusted travelers that you are strong, courageous, a good father or mother, that you have a great heart, is very powerful. Tears usually come—oh, how they want to believe it's true! Yet this is how God sees each one of us. We are merely the vessels speaking His truth to them.

When we begin to believe in ourselves, we begin to move toward a new vision of who we are, what we are becoming, and what we are going to do with our lives. Now, I am no longer running from pain to addictive behaviors to medicate my life. I am running *toward* this new vision of me. In the end, there is nothing more important than self-affirmation. Here are some positive steps to increasing self-esteem:

SURROUNDING YOURSELF WITH POSITIVE PEOPLE

You need a team of people around you who will speak positive affirmations into your life. You also need friends to hold you accountable for doing your work of visualizations and affirmations, taking care of yourself physically, and keeping your appointments. These are the people who will help you stay on track.

EXERCISING REGULARLY

I cannot overemphasize the positive effect physical activity has on self-esteem. I don't know of any other activity that has such an impact on people as becoming active and taking care of ourselves physically. You will feel better about yourself when you eat healthy, get good sleep, and become active. After about twenty or thirty minutes of aerobic activity, such as walking, swimming, biking, or jogging, the body produces endorphins that create a feeling of euphoric well-being. It's very positive and uplifting.

FAKING IT UNTIL YOU MAKE IT

In recovery, we use the phrase of "fake it till you make it." Feelings take time to change. What we tell people is to do the right thing, do the positive thing, even if you don't feel like it, even if you still feel negative. In time, the good feelings will follow, causing our perspectives to change.

REFLECTION QUESTIONS

Are you more like Manoah, who says, "Nothing good ever happens to us," or Manoah's wife, who says, "All things are possible with God." Why?

Consider the following situations and state how you would respond in each situation:

Your boss summons you to her office. Do you anticipate you're getting laid off or getting a pay raise?

Your spouse or significant other calls you at work, needing to speak with you later that night about something that has happened. Do you panic or look forward to the conversation?

To whom do you most compare yourself? Why do you think that is?

What do you think it means to be perfect?

Do you believe that you can obtain perfection? Why or why not?

Below, write a negative thought you've been having on a continual basis. Make an effort to replace that thought by crossing it out and writing a positive one in its place.

REFLECTIONS

REFLECTIONS

CHAPTER 6

MY LIFELONG PLAN
FOR POSITIVE SELF-ESTEEM

There is a story about a concert pianist named Paderewski who was giving a concert in a great auditorium. All the people had gathered, but he was delayed in coming out, and the auditorium was buzzing with anticipation. Then a little eight-year-old boy—who'd been dragged to this concert by his mother—got an idea. When his mom failed to keep tabs on him, he got up, climbed the stairs, sat down at the piano and started to play "Chopsticks," the only song he knew. Those in the auditorium began to talk among themselves about the rudeness of the incident: Where was the boy's mother? Why wasn't she retrieving her son? Get the kid out of there!

Paderewski, waiting in the wings, heard the commotion. But instead of calling the security people, he put on his tuxedo jacket, walked over to the piano, and reaching his big arms around this little boy, began to play along, masterfully improvising. Paderewski leaned over and whispered in the boy's ear: "Just one thing, son. Don't stop playing. Don't quit. Just keep going. Just keep playing. This is going to be a masterpiece. Just don't stop."

Somehow Paderewski made this looming disaster into a moment of profundity—a simple, childish song became a masterpiece. And God is like this. When we mess up, he improvises. He gets us back on the right road. We all need God to put His giant hands around our lives to create masterpieces. Without Him, our lives are juvenile concerts—not much to listen to or watch.

In this final chapter, we are going to look at a lifelong plan to nourish positive self-worth in your life. Making money, gaining recognition, or having material wealth doesn't equal positive self-worth. These are all external gains or efforts. In recovery, a person gains self-worth by living a life of significance and purpose. The greatness of Rick Warren's book, *The Purpose Driven Life*, is that it demonstrates how purpose and significance come from using our lives to benefit others. We were created by God to help others, to make a difference, to make a better world. A life focused on self always falls apart. Selfishness is an empty attempt at happiness. Like the well Christ talked about with the Samaritan woman, self-seeking will never quench our thirst:

> A woman of Samaria came to draw water. Jesus said to her, "Give Me a drink." For His disciples had gone away into the city to buy food. Then the woman of Samaria said to Him, "How is it that You, being a Jew, ask a drink from me, a Samaritan woman?" For Jews have no dealings with Samaritans.
>
> Jesus answered and said to her, "If you knew the gift of God, and who it is who says to you, 'Give Me a drink,' you would have asked Him, and He would have given you living water."
>
> The woman said to Him, "Sir, You have nothing to draw with, and the well is deep. Where then do You get that living water? Are You greater than our father Jacob, who gave us the well, and drank from it himself, as well as his sons and his livestock?"
>
> Jesus answered and said to her, "Whoever drinks of this water will thirst again, but whoever drinks of the water that I shall give

him will never thirst. But the water that I shall give him will become in him a fountain of water springing up into everlasting life."

The woman said to Him, "Sir, give me this water, that I may not thirst, nor come here to draw." (John 4:7–15 NKJV)

It was as if Jesus put His giant hands around her soul and turned her chaotic music into a masterpiece. Jesus knew the woman thirsted for spiritual water.

Maybe you've felt unhappy at some point in your life. Maybe you are unhappy right now. This low-grade depression can cause feelings of low self-worth. Sure, we won't always feel happy—life can be difficult and isn't always full of joy. But brooding unhappiness is the result of unrealistic dreams. We may feel if Prince Charming doesn't ride into our lives on a white horse, then our lives are failures. Maybe the problem is with our perception. Sometimes Prince Charming drives a Pinto or sings bad karaoke. Sometimes we fall in love with the idea of love, instead of the reality of love. Once we do this, our happiness depends on the fulfillment of these unrealistic dreams.

There's a great story about Charles Steinmetz, an electrical engineering genius who worked for General Electric in the early part of the twentieth century. On one occasion after his retirement, the company called him in because the other engineers were baffled about the breakdown of a complex of machines. They asked Charles to pinpoint the problem. He walked around the machines for a while, then took a piece of chalk from his pocket and made a big cross mark on a specific point of one particular machine. To their amazement, when the engineers disassembled that part of the machine, it turned out to be the precise location of the breakdown.

A few days later, the engineers received a bill from Charles for ten thousand dollars—a staggering sum in those days. They returned the bill and asked him to itemize it. His response read:

Making one cross mark: $1.00
Knowing where to put it: $9,999.00

Changing our lives always starts with putting the cross mark on the
right spot. This is the work of pre-contemplation. Gerald May writes,
"How much can I respect myself if I do not even know what I really
want?"[1] I'll add, "How can I change if I haven't identified the problem?"
This is what Jesus did for the woman at the well. He helped her put an
X on the spot where she ached the most. Then He gave her a solution—
living water. Whatever it is that we want, living water is at the heart of
it. We have a basic need in our soul for this water that only Christ can
offer. Commentator William Barclay writes, "She was suddenly com-
pelled to face herself and the looseness and immorality and total inadequacy of her life. There are two revelations in Christianity: the
revelation of God and the revelation of ourselves. . . . We awake to ourselves and we awake to our need of God."[2]

We would tend to think this type of revelation would tear down self-
worth, but the reality is quite the opposite. One of the reasons people in
recovery begin to build self-worth is because they start the process of
self-denial. If life is all about me, then I'm going to wallow in self-centeredness. This is where we usually struggle with low self-esteem. We
must focus on using our gifts and talents to the benefit of others if we
are going to build self-worth. Our focus should turn outward instead of
inward. This revelation has given me a strong sense of purpose. I wake
up every morning embracing my life and trying to use it for others.
With this comes a sense of self-respect and even a compassion for
myself.

The image we project to the world should be the same person we
are in private. When we are honest with ourselves first, not pretend-
ing to be someone we're not, we show self-respect. Until we find the
X that marks the spot of our brokenness, we're deceiving ourselves,
and that keeps us from relating to ourselves just as we relate to
Christ.

Melissa's Story

" . . . He who has begun a good work in you will complete it . . . "
—Phil. 1:6 NKJV

"Spiritually I'm in a good place. I was always a doer, thinking I had to do, do, do for God. I've grown out of that. God already loves me. He already cares about me. He's already set a plan for me. I can't screw that up by not going to church or not reading my Bible enough. He loves me regardless. And the desire to do those things comes from that. Reading, serving—I want to do these things for Someone who loves me.

"Mentally, I'm doing well. I'm not so hard on myself, and I'm working on not being so hard on my husband, expecting him to fulfill all my needs. I'm learning more about myself—what I like and who I am.

"Physically, things have been tough because I do suffer from a food addiction. I'm now at one of the highest weights I've ever been, and it's a struggle with toxic shame, thinking that I'm so far gone—is it even worth it? But I keep going back to the fact that I want to do this for myself. I'm in that place now—I really want to get healthy, and I'm working hard at doing that. I haven't totally overcome my negative self-image, but I'm working on transforming that into a positive self-assessment. That's where I am today. It's the grace and mercy of God that has brought me through this. He's still with me. He's still present. He gets me through every day."

Here is a great formula for successful growth: Consistency + time + grace = growth. Consistency is practicing a new way of doing things. As we talked about in the *Journey to Freedom Manual*, consistency means putting yourself in a position to do the right thing, even if you do not feel like it. Do the right thing now and your feelings will catch up. Consistently speak positive affirmations to yourself, even if you have a hard time feeling as if they are true.

This may be a difficult process if you have been telling yourself damaging things for years, so consistency is key. Practicing the new behavior daily, and the new, positive voice that you need to hear will emerge.

Time is the second part of the formula. Sometimes people don't give themselves enough time to change, but you must have patience. For many of us, this process will continue for the rest of our lives. The goal is not perfection—it is progress.

The last component of the formula is grace. Grace is the most powerful force in the universe. Grace is compassion for self, allowing yourself to move forward and sometimes backward. Grace is God's unconditional love for each of us. In the Bible, Paul says that nothing "will be able to separate us from the love of God" (Rom. 8:39 NIV). If you consistently speak these affirmations, and continue to live in the grace of God, you *will* change. You will begin to believe in who He says that you are.

There's psychological research demonstrating how positive self-talk determines whether or not we succeed when faced with difficulty. Psychologist Martin Seligman writes in *Learned Optimism*:

> Your way of explaining events to yourself determines how helpless you can become, or how energized, when you encounter the everyday setbacks as well as momentous defeats. I think of your explanatory style as reflecting "the word in your heart."
>
> Each of us carries a word in his heart, a "no" or a "yes." You probably don't know intuitively which word lives there, but you can learn, with a fair degree of accuracy, which it is.... The first step is to discover the word in your heart.[3]

Seligman says the word in your heart can be discovered by the way you view your difficulties. A pessimistic person believes that bad events will last a long time. The pessimist also interprets bad events as his or her own fault, whereas an optimistic person sees defeat as a temporary setback. Seligman says that "optimists believe defeat is not their fault: Circumstances, bad luck, or other people brought it about. Such people are unfazed by defeat. Confronted by a bad situation, they perceive it as a challenge and try harder."[4] It's Seligman's belief that we can change our explanatory style by what we tell ourselves about our situations.

YOU CAN CHANGE YOUR ATTITUDE

Believe it or not, you can change your attitude! The following ideas will help you convert your perspective from negative to positive.

Stay away from toxic relationships. Negative and cynical people are like poison. They pull us down and suck the life out of everyone around them. I once heard a local minister refer to negative people as black-hole people. Many times, they have low self-worth. We need to be surrounded by people who are going to inspire us and lift our spirits.

This is why the YMCA is such a wonderful place. Walking into the Y every day, I feel a burst of positive energy. People are there to improve their lives spiritually, physically, and mentally. If I feel empty after a long day at work, I don't go to a bar and drink. I go lift weights or take a swim class with others. I need that positive environment. When I leave the YMCA, I feel positive about myself—and that increases my self-worth. When I leave a bar, I leave feeling negative because I've chosen to drown in my problems instead of work through them.

So choose your friends wisely, and surround yourself with optimistic people. The people you choose to fill your life will have a major impact on it—either positive or negative.

Stay in community and out of isolation. Attending church is a positive, uplifting experience. Seligman writes, "Organized religion provides a belief that there is more good to life than meets the eye. Failures of individuals are buffered by belief in being part of a much larger whole: Buffering takes place whether the hope is concrete as a golden afterlife or as abstract as being part of God's plan."[5] The opposite of community is isolation. It's easy to fall into a dangerous downward spiral when we isolate ourselves. Isolation provides fertile ground for pessimism. The solution is to become a part of a community. Find a group of people who will help pull you out of isolation.

God will do for us what we cannot do for ourselves. One of the greatest gifts God has given me in rebuilding my self-worth is the understanding that I'm not perfect. I tend to be disorganized at times. Sometimes I'm not very efficient. I have a hard time staying focused for long periods of time. I have a lot of weaknesses. But I also have a lot of strengths. I'm passionate, articulate, and well-read. I work well with people and have the ability to cast a vision. In the past, I would have focused on my imperfections, constantly berating myself for falling short. Then I realized God could do for me what I couldn't do for myself. This is where the serenity prayer comes in: *God grant me the serenity to accept the things I cannot change, courage to change the things I can, and wisdom to know the difference.*

Time and time again, God has brought people into my life who can do for me what I can't do for myself. It feels great when people help me and together we accomplish something that I could never have accomplished alone. I have learned to swallow my pride and say, "Could you please help me?" This has been a huge lesson for me. We must acknowledge our weaknesses and allow God to do for us what we cannot do for ourselves. Possessing this type of wisdom builds our sense of self-worth.

REFLECTION QUESTIONS

Have you ever conjured up a set of expectations of how things should be in your life? Tell of a time when you had unrealistic expectations of a situation in your life.

Describe how it might feel to have Jesus's arms around you, helping you turn the clumsy music of your life into a masterpiece. Would you feel worthy or embarrassed? Why?

It seems that the woman at the well was unhappy about something in her life. Have you ever felt unhappy with your life? What did you do about it?

If you had to place an X on one of the areas below where you most need to fix your life, where would you place it and why? Put an X over one of the areas below or come up with your own.

Relationships – Personal Struggle – Marriage – Parenthood – Finances –Purpose–

*Career Choice –*_____ *(Other)*

Do you think you have a pessimistic or an optimistic point of view? Explain.

Do you believe that a pessimistic person can become optimistic? How?

REFLECTIONS

REFLECTIONS

REFLECTIONS

MY PERSONAL PLAN OF CHANGE

SAMPLE PLAN OF CHANGE

Read through the following sample Personal Plan of Change before completing your own plan.

> Self Assessment: My name is Sally. I am a forty-year-old housewife with three children. I have always struggled with low self-worth. My weight is normal, but I always feel as though I am overweight. I am very codependent, and I struggle with feeling good about myself. I am always concerned about what my husband and children think of me. On occasions, I have struggled with an eating disorder of binging and purging while working out all the time. I am never satisfied with how I am spiritually, mentally, and physically. I have also dealt with mild depression for several years.

Step One
Spirit: I am a beautiful daughter of God.
Friend says: Sally has the most beautiful spirit and is such a lovely woman of God.

Mind: I am a wonderful mother and wife.
Friend says: Sally is such a courageous and devoted mother and wife.

Body: I am a beautiful woman with a very healthy body.

Friend says: Sally has one of the most beautiful smiles of anyone I know. She lights up a room with it.

Step Two

Spirit: During my daily quiet time, I will speak my daily affirmation aloud in the presence of God. I will also find verses in the Bible that reflect God's truth about who He says I am.

Mind: I will take five to ten minutes a day to meditate on my affirmations, visualizing being that person.

Body: I will go for a thirty- to sixty-minute walk three to five times a week and meditate on my affirmations while doing aerobic activity.

Step Three

Support Community:
  Women's group at church
  Weight Watchers

Individual support:
  Heather (my best friend)
  My accountability partner from my twelve-step group
  Debbie, head of Women's Ministries at church
  Heidi, my work out partner

Step Four

I will believe in myself and in my self-worth. I will not obsess about my body and food. I will not be dependent on my husband and children to feel good about myself. I will live in a freedom of the knowledge that I am beloved child of God. That belief will free me to truly love my husband and children. I will enjoy my life so much more because I will not be living with the constant worry of whether or not I am good enough. I will accept my strengths and weaknesses, knowing that I do not have to be perfect. I will be more relaxed. I will have more to offer others. I will no longer give to get. I will live out of abundance. I will love who I am.

Step Five

Lord, I have lived in shame and self-isolation for so long because, deep down, I do not believe that I am worthy. I have refused to let anyone love me—including You—because of my fear of being rejected. Lord, please help me let go of these negative thoughts and beliefs that I have about myself. Help me to see myself the way that You see me. Help me to know that You have created me just as I am. I want to trust You to change me from the inside out because I am powerless to do anything on my own might. I know that You have great plans for my life. Help me to be defined by Your standards and not my own. Thank You, Lord. Amen.

CREATING YOUR PERSONAL PLAN OF CHANGE

Step One

You are going to create a daily plan of action to build positive self-worth. You will practice daily affirmations and visualizations that will begin to foster a new belief about who you are. Prepare to affirm yourself from a spirit, mind, and body perspective. Under each of the following headings, write positive affirmations about yourself. Then, find a couple of very close friends or sponsors, and have them write five positive affirmations about you from their perspective.

Examples:

Spirit: "I am a cherished and beloved child of God."

Mind: "I am a capable, intelligent person."

Body: "I have beautiful, sparkling blue eyes that are full of life."

Spirit:

Mind:

Body:

Other affirmations:

Step Two

Practice specific steps to meet your goals:

Read your affirmations aloud daily.

On a weekly basis, meet with a support group, pastor, friend, or family member and share your affirmations. Receive affirmation back from your support person on your statements.

Put your written statements on a note card and place it in your wallet, on your bathroom mirror, in your car, at your desk, or any-where that allows you to visualize these statements multiple times throughout the day.

As more positive statements come to mind, jot them down with the other affirmations. Regularly read these and share them with others.

In addition, consider exercises that will affirm your spirit, mind, and body. For example:

Spirit: Schedule daily time to pray and read your Bible or a spiritually-centered book.

Mind: Take some time to be alone. Close your eyes and meditate, visualizing yourself possessing the qualities you have written down.

Body: Three to five times a week, take a daily walk or bike ride for an hour. Use that time to focus and meditate on your affirma-tion cards.

Step Three

Find a support team.

1. Find a support community. (Choose one of the options below or another group that suits you)

   Restore Ministries (www.restoreymca.org)
   Alcoholics Anonymous (www.alcoholics-anonymous.org)
   Overeaters Anonymous (www.oa.org)
   Al Anon (www.al-anon.org)
   Narcotics Anonymous (www.na.org)

2. Find individuals to support you. (List some individuals below who can support you on this journey.)

   Friend:
   Sponsor:
   Therapist:
   Counselor/Doctor:
   Pastor:
   Life Coach:
   Personal Trainer/Nutritionist/Physical Therapist:
   Other:

Step Four

Write a brief description of how you will see yourself once you begin to believe your statements of affirmation to be true.

Step Five

Finding a sense of self-worth begins by finding strength in Christ. Below, write a prayer that you can say every day while you are working through your journey toward recognizing your self-worth.

CONCLUSION

I believe that low self-worth is the greatest plague of modern man. It is chronic. Almost everyone that we have worked with in our Restore Ministries small groups has struggled with low self-worth. It doesn't seem to matter if we're dealing with a successful attorney, a doctor, or an unemployed high school dropout—low self-worth is an equal-opportunity tormenter. It causes its victims to medicate their lives with a variety of drugs and addictive behaviors, and often this destruction is passed on to their children. Coming to believe that we are who God says we really are, and living in the freedom and strength of that positive self-worth, is the key to fulfillment in our lives.

Mike Bynum, author of *Bear Bryant's Boys of Autumn*, writes:

> I realized then that even though the years may whirl past faster than we can often know or realize, and where we were and where we may one day be, is always separated by a blurring, fading vortex of half-remembrances and budding dreams of glory, and yes, these images are really colored by sun, not shadow. Camelot, therefore, is not just a mythical kingdom in some mythical world, instead, it is the gifted ability of inner vision to see what we'd rather see and to become what we'd rather be.[1]

God bless you on your journey.

TIPS FOR LEADING A JOURNEY TO FREEDOM SMALL GROUP

Welcome and thank you for accepting the challenge of leading others along their own journeys to freedom. These tips are designed to aid you in creating a small group setting that is productive and full of hope, health, and happiness.

PREPARATION

Being well prepared will help alleviate any anxiety you may have about leading your group. When you know what you want to accomplish in your group, it will help you stay on track with the lesson plan. Plus, if you're not prepared, participants will pick up on your lack of preparation, which might affect their own dedication to the group and the process of change. In extreme cases, lack of preparation may even cause you to lose some participants. If the leader is not committed, why should the participants be committed? So come to your group prepared to lead them.

Be a role model. A good facilitator is simply a model group participant. Be on time. Be prepared. Do your homework. Guard against moodiness.

Be consistent. Be positive. Be a good listener. Maintain confidentiality. Be enthusiastic.

Recognize your limitations. It is important that you remember that you are not responsible for the results of your group. You are not responsible to "fix" anyone. You are not a counselor, a therapist, or a minister. You are a mentor, one who is helping guide another down a path that you have traveled before. Each participant is responsible for his or her own life and journey.

OPENING THE GROUP SESSION

Use gentleness and patience as you pace the progress of the group. Rushing through the lessons might be exhausting for your participants. Try to find some kind of meaningful devotional, excerpt from a book, or song to emphasize and complement what you are studying for the week.

Plan your time so that you are able to get through the majority of the recommended questions in each less on, but more important, be prepared to settle for quality of questions and answers over quantity. The goal is to have a productive meeting. Getting through every question in the lesson may seem optimal, but it may not accomplish the goal.

BE AWARE

Avoid being the center of attention during group time. Your role as leader is to get the group involved in sharing, to keep the discussion moving forward and on topic, and to make sure that your group is on time and the necessary material is covered. You are there to give direction and guidance to the group, but avoid dominating the group by talking too much in the sessions.

Be aware of your group dynamics. As a facilitator, get to know your group members. In order to help them as much as possible, you need to be aware and in tune with their needs. Pay attention to the members' body language, their actions, and what they are saying and sharing. Assess the participants in their response and in their openness (or lack of).

Don't let any one member dominate the group. Handling the "talker" in your group will require some skill. Be careful, because if one member begins to dominate your group, it can alienate some of the more reserved members. If one member is opening up and sharing for long periods of time, try not to let this member's problems control the group. Say, "I would love to continue this discussion with you after the meeting. Will that be okay?" This will keep you from appearing uncaring and will give the group permission to get back on track. Also, think about positioning. Sit beside these individuals instead of across from them to avoid prolonged eye contact. When presenting a question or topic for discussion, put a time limit on responses. If someone runs over the limit, don't be afraid to break in and praise the person's point, but then raise a new question back to the group about what was shared. Validate the individual's feelings and input, but then focus the discussion.

Allow silence. Often, facilitators become uncomfortable with silence in group discussions. Sometimes it is good to have a moment of silence so that the participants will speak up and start owning the conversation. Do not feel like you have to fill the void. If the group members think you are going to fill the silence, then they will learn to wait for you. If you find that there has been a considerable amount of time given to answer a question and no one is speaking up, you might ask them why they are silent or move on to another question.

Contain the desire to rescue. If someone gets emotionally upset or begins to cry and show emotion during the session, avoid anything that could interfere with the member feeling the emotion of the moment. Let the individual express the emotions and deal with them, even if they are painful. While the person is sharing, do not reach over and hug, touch, or comfort. After the individual has finished sharing and is done, then offer a hug if you desire or thank and affirm the person for speaking courageously.

Use self-disclosure appropriately. One element of being a good facilitator is a willingness to be vulnerable and to share your journey of change at the appropriate times. However, be careful that you do not use the group to deal with your unresolved issues.

As you lead discussion, consistently state and reiterate the boundaries of group discussion—confidentiality about what is spoken in the group, respect for each other, and the right to pass if a member doesn't feel comfortable sharing at the time. Accept what each person has to say without making sudden judgments. Be the primary catalyst in providing a warm, open, trusting, and caring atmosphere. This will help the group gradually take ownership.

CLOSING THE GROUP

Manage your time wisely. It is important that your group start and end on time. Strive for consistency, beginning with the first meeting by starting and ending on time and continuing that schedule each week.

SESSION ONE—INTRODUCTION WEEK

Lesson Goal:

In your first meeting you will not cover any material. You will begin to get to know each other as a group and learn the structure and guidelines for the next eight weeks, as well as the expectations of each participant.

Leading the Session:

Welcome the participants and commend them on taking this action to pursue change in their lives.

Ask each participant to share whatever information they are

comfortable sharing about themselves with the group: name, occupation, number and ages of children and or grandchildren, where you were born, how you heard of this group, etc. are good places to start. Be sure that you and your co-facilitator (if applicable) introduce yourselves first to increase the group's comfort level.

Show the first session of Scott Reall's video (if applicable), talk about what they have to look forward to as a group in the upcoming eight weeks, and present group guidelines to the participants:

Confidentiality is of the utmost importance.
Group members are not required to talk but encouraged to do so.
Agree to accept each other and to encourage one another.
We do not give advice, or try to "fix" or rescue other group members.
Be honest.
Be on time.
Agree to make the weekly meetings and the daily work a priority.

Ask if anyone would like to ask a question or add a group guideline. The goal is for participants to feel safe, secure and encouraged.

Choose one of the following warm-up questions to open up the group and begin to break the ice:

What do you like to do when you have free time?
What brings you great joy?
What is a special talent or skill that you possess?

Pair your group into couples, and give each person five minutes to answer the following questions to each other:

What brought you here today?
What in your life do you want to change?
What excuses will you give yourself to not come to group or do your homework?

Closing the Group

Encourage the group members to come back to the next meeting.

Encourage group members to read and answer the questions at the end of the chapter to be discussed next week and to write their answers in the blank space provided. Tell them to come next week ready to discuss.

Assign accountability partners for each participant and, if possible, pair them with the partner that they were paired with for the last exercise. Ask them to exchange phone numbers and e-mail addresses.

Accountability Partner Guidelines:

Discuss the specifics of the change each person is trying to achieve.

Relate how each person is doing in spirit, mind, and body.

Ask your partner about his or her struggles, problems, and particular difficulties.

Be considerate of each other's time and situations, and remember that the purpose is to discuss change.

Make an effort to take the conversation beyond a superficial level.

The Importance of Accountability Partners:

One of the best tools to help us through the rough times in our journey to freedom is accountability. Often we don't realize how much accountability has influenced and affected our decisions throughout our lives. We are accountable to get to work on time or we may lose our jobs. In school, athletes have to keep their grades up, attend class, and get to practice or they are off the team. In the same way, unless we have some sort of accountability, many of us will not sustain our efforts to change. We need accountability to develop the discipline of sticking with something, especially if consistency is hard for us.

Be sure and thank them for coming this week. Express how excited you are to be with them and to discover where this journey is going to take all of you as a group.

Close with prayer, singing, saying the serenity prayer, or any positive way you feel appropriate.

SESSIONS 2 THROUGH 7—COVERING THE STUDY GUIDE MATERIAL

For these six weeks, you will be covering Chapters 1 through 6 in the study guide. You will want to follow and review the guidelines for preparing for leading a small group. Once each session begins thank everyone for being there and then begin to go over that week's readings and have members share about what stood out to them in the lesson. You will then want to go over the questions at the end of the chapter for the rest of your time. If some do not want to share their answers, do not force them. Thank everyone that shares for participating and encourage those that don't. Encourage members to use the Reflection pages at he end of each chapter during the week for journaling and notes. End in prayer.

SESSION 8—CREATING PERSONAL PLANS OF CHANGE

Leading the Session:

Go over the group guidelines for respecting participants as they share their plans.

Have participants read action plans aloud.

Have them sign the places provided in their books, committing them to follow the plans of action they have created.

Talk about the specific next steps that they can take (for example, enrolling in a twelve-steps or other recovery program or a personal training or exercise program).

Make sure they have all the resources they need to fulfill their action plans.

Thank them for coming and close in prayer.

Hold hands and sing "Amazing Grace."

NOTES

Introduction
1. Not her real name.
2. Dr. Paul Tournier, *The Strong and the Weak*, trans. Edwin Hudson (Philadelphia: The WestMinster Press, 1963), 21.

Chapter 1
1. Proverbs 23:7 NKJV.
2. John Ortberg, *The Life You've Always Wanted*, (Grand Rapids, Mich.: Zondervan, 1997), 42.
3. Ibid, 42.

Chapter 2
1. Robert S. McGee, *The Search for Significance*, (Nashville: Word Publishing, 1998), iii.
2. David Foster Wallace, *Oblivion*, (New York: Little, Brown, and Company), 147.
3. John Bradshaw, *Healing the Shame That Binds You (revised)*, (Deerfield Beach, FL: Health Communications, 2005), vii.
4. McGee, 36.
5. C. S. Lewis, *Mere Christianity*, (New York: Harcourt, 1996), 87.
6. Aaron T. Beck, *Prisoners of Hate: The Cognitive Basis of Anger, Hostility, and Violence*, (New York: HarperCollins, 1999), 27.
7. Lewis, 87.

Chapter 3
1. Proverbs 29:18 KJV.
2. Harry Emerson Fosdick, *On Being a Real Person*, (New York: Harper Brothers, 1943), 86–87.
3. Howard Culbertson, "No Reserves. No Retreats. No Regrets.", Southern Nazarene University, http://home.snu.edu/~HCULBERT/regret.htm (accessed May 3, 2007).
4. Richard Yates, *Revolutionary Road*, (New York: Vintage Books, 2000), 77–80.

Chapter 4
1. Michael Green, *Illustrations for Biblical Preaching*, (Grand Rapids, Mich.: Baker Books, 1991), 328–329.
2. Dr. Gerald May, *Addictions and Grace*, (San Francisco: HarperSanFrancisco, 1991), 31.
3. C. S. Lewis, *The Four Loves*, (New York: Harcourt, 1988), 3.
4. James S. Hewett, ed., *Illustrations Unlimited*, (Wheaton, Ill.: Tyndale, 1988), 296.

Chapter 5
1. Arthur Freeman and Rose DeWolf, *Woulda, Coulda, Shoulda*, 41.

Chapter 6

1. Gerald May, *Addiction & Grace*, (San Francisco: HarperSanFrancisco, 1991), 42.
2. William Barclay, *The Book of John, Vol. 1*, (Philadelphia, Penn.: Westminster Press, 1975), 156–157.
3. Martin Seligman, *Learned Optimism*, (New York: Pocket Books, 1992), 16.
4. Ibid, 4–5.
5. Ibid, 203.

Conclusion

1. Mike Bynum, *Bear Bryant's Boys of Autumn*, (High Tide Autumn Football Ltd, 1987), 229.